FINGERBOARD WORKBOOK
FOR THE THIRD POSITION

Map the Viola for Good
by Diane Allen

ISBN-978-1470106560

The Fingerboard Workbook Series

by Diane Allen

VIOLIN:

Fingerboard Workbook for the First Position: Map the Violin for Good

Fingerboard Workbook for the Second Position: Map the Violin for Good

Fingerboard Workbook for the Third Position: Map the Violin for Good

Fingerboard Workbook for the Fourth Position: Map the Violin for Good

Fingerboard Workbook for the Fifth and Sixth Positions: Map the Violin for Good

Fingerboard Workbook for the Seventh and Eighth Positions: Map the Violin for Good

Fingerboard Workbook for the Ninth, Tenth, and Eleventh Positions: Map the Violin for Good

VIOLA:

Fingerboard Workbook for the First Position: Map the Viola for Good

Fingerboard Workbook for the Second Position: Map the Viola for Good

Fingerboard Workbook for the Third Position: Map the Viola for Good

Fingerboard Workbook for the Fourth Position: Map the Viola for Good

Fingerboard Workbook for the Fifth and Sixth Positions: Map the Viola for Good

Fingerboard Workbook for the Seventh and Eighth Positions: Map the Viola for Good

Fingerboard Workbook for the Ninth, Tenth, and Eleventh Positions: Map the Viola for Good

Although the series can be done in any order, it is strongly recommended that you begin with first position to lay the foundation for the rest of the series. Essential Background Information is explained on a video tutorial which can be found at www.fingerboardworkbookseries.com.

Table of Contents

Acknowledgements

I would like to extend my deep gratitude to many people who have enriched my life in wonderful ways. Those mentioned here have had a direct influence with regard to creating *The Fingerboard Workbook Series*.

BURTON KAPLAN, Professor of Violin at The Manhattan School of Music, introduced me to fingerboard visualization. I'll never forget those first "aha moments" and making sense of the fingerboard! The fingerboard chart I have used in this workbook is very similar to the one found in his books, *The Complete Music Sight-Reader Series*.

LARRY SNIDER, Head of the Percussion Department at the University of Akron, introduced me to Neuro-Linguistic Programming and the world of "thinking out of the box."

MY HUNDREDS OF STUDENTS, who have been so passionate and eager to learn the violin. They've been amazingly open, willing participants to all my experimenting in teaching.

DILLON SCHNEIDER, Executive Director of The Cascade School of Music, for hiring me year after year to teach Fingerboard Geography and Bow Arm Boot Camp.

LAYLA McGLONE, JEAN FRYE, LESLIE BISHKO, JIM FRANCO, my village of editors, each of whom have added their special touch.

LESLIE KNIGHT, my viola editor, whose musical enthusiasm is extremely contagious.

PHILIP McDANIEL, of Profile Light Design, has transformed and uplifted the look and layout of *The Fingerboard Workbook Series*. Thanks for making my work look great on paper!

JOHN ALLEN, my husband, who has spent countless hours helping me brainstorm creative and effective ways to teach and communicate.

Introduction

Is it a coincidence or karma that Hindemith's Mathis der Maler happens to be the music I'm learning while assembling *The Fingerboard Workbook Series?* The first violin part covers 1st – 11th positions. One measure has all flats, the next all sharps. I've been identifying with my eyes many 3rds, 4ths and 5ths and hearing them in my head before playing. I've been drilling spots so my hand remembers the finger patterns of what these seemingly strange notes feel like. The music has layers of pencil that have been erased and penciled over again only to be erased again: a testimony of the many violinists who have attempted to do their best to learn such a challenging piece of music.

My friends will tell you how I griped, and groaned while learning Mathis der Maler. What they don't know is that once I got over the initial shock of what it took for me to learn the piece, that I enjoyed the process with immense satisfaction! From Fb's to B#'s, 11th position to 2nd, I've been able to see, hear, and feel my way through the learning process.

Learning this piece of music has strengthened my resolve in completing *The Fingerboard Workbook Series*. Mathis der Maler provided a great "real world test" for *The Fingerboard Workbook Series*, and I am excited to report that it passed with flying colors!

If you have completed *Fingerboard Workbook for the First Position: Map the Viola for Good*, then you are prepared to forge ahead. It does not matter which order you complete the rest of the books in *The Fingerboard Workbook Series*.

If you are unfamiliar to this series, or have not completed *Fingerboard Workbook for the First Position: Map the Viola for Good*, then let me get you up to speed on some background you will need to fill out the workbook. If this seems like too much, go back and get all your basics with *Fingerboard Workbook for the First Position: Map the Viola for Good*.

Here is a list of pre-requisites you will need to fill out this workbook:
- Know how to read notes
- Know how to read the sharps and flats in the key signature
- Have a general concept of finding notes on the viola
- Understanding of the charts and maps in the section: Essential Background Information
- Have a full understanding of half steps and whole steps

(Tutorial available at: www.fingerboardworkbookseries.com)

What will be possible for you? What music will become available to you? How will confidence in fingerboard geography serve you? Jump into *The Fingerboard Workbook Series* and find out! Sharpen your pencil, sharpen your ears, and sharpen your mind!

Diane Allen

7

MASTER FINGERBOARD

The Third Position

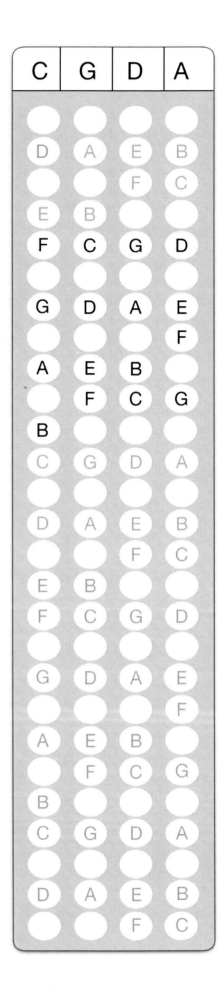

Essential Background Information

In order to fill out the workbook, students must be familiar with the order of notes and how to determine half steps and whole steps. You can gain a basic understanding of this information by viewing the Essential Background video tutorial on www.fingerboardworkbookseries.com. Knowing the order of notes, half steps and whole steps is an integral part of laying the foundation for mapping the fingerboard. Once you have a basic understanding, the act of filling out the workbook will drill the concepts to memorization and mastery.

The Keyboard/Fingerboard Chart is for reference while filling out the workbook. You will find a copy of this on page 13 and a PDF download on www.fingerboardworkbookseries.com. Use the Keyboard for a quick reference of where the notes are and their distances from each other. The Fingerboard Chart is currently filled out with the following items:

• The circles show where the notes exist and are spaced one half step apart

• The letters represent where the natural notes are in this position

• The numbers represent finger numbers

• The letters next to the numbers are: L – Low, H - High, X - Extra

I use a very traditional fingering method. If a "D" is played with a 3rd finger, then a "Db" is played with 3L (3rd finger low) and "D#" is played with 3H (3rd finger high). Same letter = same finger.

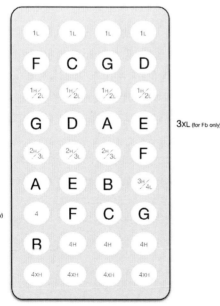

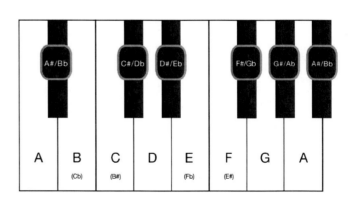

You will begin each section with identification and mapping, then actually experience the music by singing and playing. Each section concludes with a summary of the material and review.

HOW TO WRITE IN THE WORKBOOK – IDENTIFICATION AND MAPPING

On the next page you will find an example of how to fill out the written part of this workbook. When filling out each exercise use the following order.

MUSICAL EXAMPLE:

1 . Key Signature*

2 . Note Names

FINGERBOARD CHART**:

3 . Note Names

4 . Finger Numbers

MUSICAL EXAMPLE:

5 . Finger Numbers

6 . Interval***

*Key Signature

Students will reinforce key signature reading by writing down each sharp or flat from left to right. For example: Key Signature Bb, Eb, Ab. (With young students I wait to teach the names of the key signatures. If you prefer you can include: Eb Major and c minor.)

**Fingerboard Chart

Refer to your Keyboard/Fingerboard Chart on page 13 when filling out the blank fingerboard charts. You can also download the chart from www.fingerboardworkbookseries.com. If you have tapes on your viola fingerboard, you may want to duplicate where they are on the workbook for a direct point of reference. A highlighter works great for this.

***Interval

An interval is the distance between two notes. At the beginning of each part you will find additional instructions for identifying intervals.

Example

Key Signature __Bb Eb (Bb Major or g minor)__

Bb Eb

Interval __Mi3__

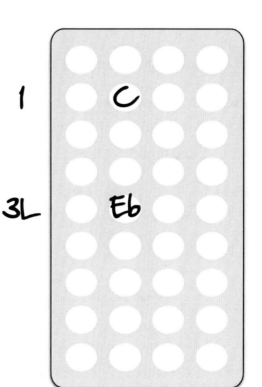

1   C

3L   Eb

C   Eb
1   3L

Key Signature __C Major or a minor__

Interval __P4__

D   G

1   4

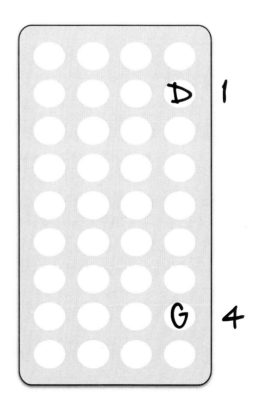

D   1

G   4

HOW TO SING AND PLAY THE EXERCISES - EXPERIENCE

Now that the written information is filled out, it's time to experience! The experience will be visual, aural and kinesthetic. We begin with singing and then playing. Make sure to use a tuner or instrument to help you find the first note.

Sing while looking at the fingerboard chart:

- Sing note names
- Sing finger numbers

Sing while looking at the musical example:

- Sing note names
- Sing finger numbers

Now you are ready to play the notes on your viola.

Play while looking at the fingerboard chart:

- Eyes will track each filled in circle

Play while looking at the musical example:

- Eyes will track each note head on the staff

HOW TO SUMMARIZE AND REVIEW

This workbook is broken down into eight parts. At the end of each part you will have three questions to answer:

- A description of what the musical example looks like
- The second will be a list of fingerings that you used
- Finally, there will be a description of the sound

Once you have completed these three questions, you will go back and play through the part noticing all the correlations that you've made in your three questions. Observe how the notes on the staff look, how you're using your fingerings, and how the sound matches your description.

When you complete the entire book, go through and play it all over again!

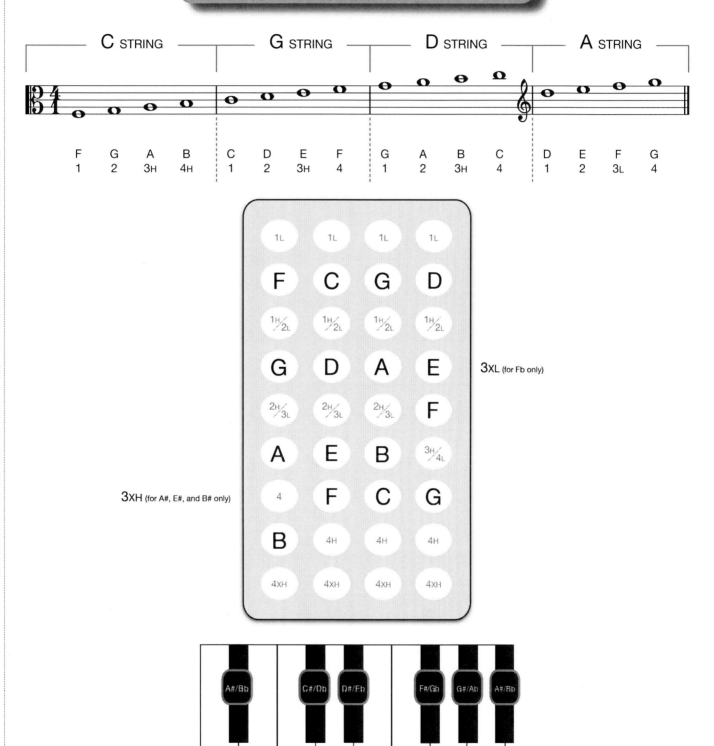

PART ONE

Half Steps and Whole Steps

Part 1 – Half Steps and Whole Steps

Half steps and whole steps are the violist's first building blocks to mapping out the entire viola. Half steps and whole steps are completely explained on the video tutorial (www.fingerboardworkbookseries.com). Make sure you have this "Essential Background Information" before you begin.

HALF STEPS AND WHOLE STEPS SHARE TWO THINGS:

• Letters in the alphabet will be next to each other (Ex.: D–E, F#–G, Bb–C)

• You will use two fingers next to each other. (Ex: 1–2, 2–3, 3–4)

HALF STEPS

• Two fingers will almost be touching

• Two circles on the fingerboard directly next to each other

• Can also be called a minor second (mi2)

WHOLE STEPS

• Two fingers with a space between

• Skip one circle on the fingerboard between the two circles used

• Can also be called a major second (Ma2)

Mark all half steps in the musical example with the half step sign: ^

Key Signature _____

Key Signature _____

Key Signature _____

Key Signature _____

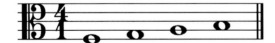

Key Signature _____

Key Signature _____

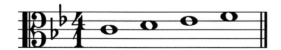

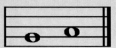

Key Signature _____

Key Signature _____

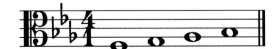

Key Signature _____

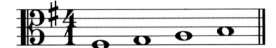

Key Signature _____

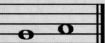

Key Signature _____

Key Signature _____

Key Signature _____

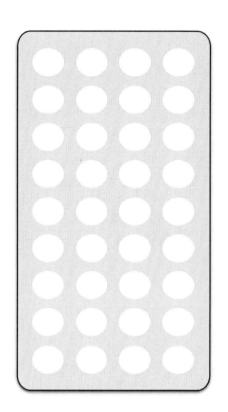

Key Signature _____

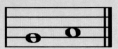

Key Signature _____

Key Signature _____

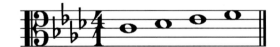

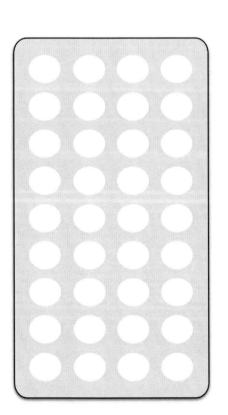

Key Signature _____

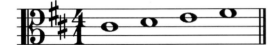

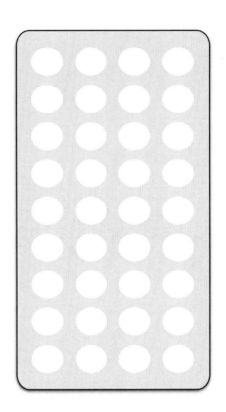

Key Signature _____

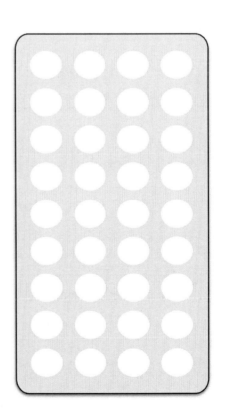

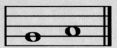
Key Signature _____

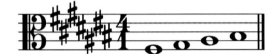

Key Signature _____

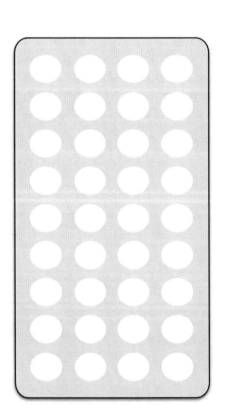

Key Signature _____

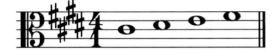

Key Signature _____

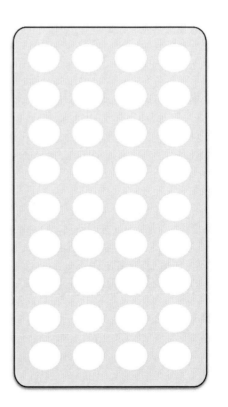

Key Signature _____

Key Signature _____

Key Signature _____

Key Signature _____

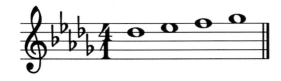

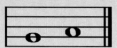

Key Signature _____

Key Signature _____

Key Signature _____

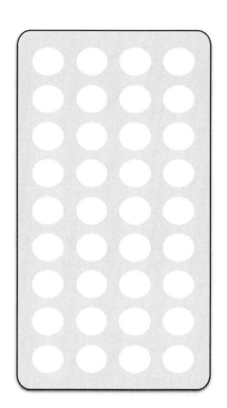

Key Signature _____

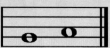
Key Signature _____

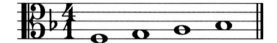

Part 1: Half Steps and Whole Steps

REVIEW QUESTIONS:

1) Describe how the notes look on the music staff. Are they on lines? Spaces? What is the distance between the lines and/or spaces?

   Example: Line to line skipping over one line or space to space skipping over one space.

2) Catalog all the fingerings you used in this part. Notice patterns.

3) Describe how the intervals sound to you. Use references to moods, descriptions or songs you recognize.

   Example: Hollow sounding reminds me of the Star Wars theme song.

REVIEW EXERCISE:

Go back and replay all the examples in Part 1 noticing:
- How the interval looks on the staff
- How the fingerings form the intervals
- How the intervals sound like your description

PART TWO

Chromatics

Chromatics are scales made up of all half steps (mi2).

USE THE SAME FINGER FOR THE SAME LETTER.

Eb - E on the A string would be fingered 2L - 2

G - G# on the D string would be fingered 1 - 1H

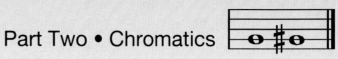

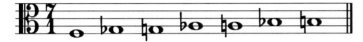

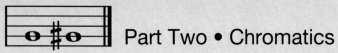 Part Two • Chromatics

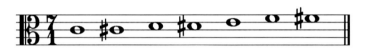

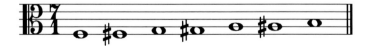

 38

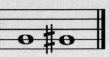

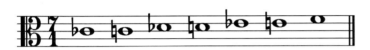

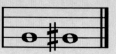

Part 2: Chromatics

REVIEW QUESTIONS:

1) Describe how the notes look on the music staff. Are they on lines? Spaces? What is the distance between the lines and/or spaces?

2) Catalog all the fingerings you used in this part. Notice patterns.

3) Describe how the interval sounds to you. Use references to moods, descriptions or songs you recognize.

REVIEW EXERCISE:

Go back and replay all the examples in Part 2 noticing:
- How the interval looks on the staff
- How the fingerings form the intervals
- How the intervals sound like your description

PART THREE

Thirds

Thirds are three notes apart. You will have two different sizes of thirds.

MINOR THIRDS (mi3):

- Half step larger than a whole step
- Half step smaller than major thirds (Ma3)

MAJOR THIRDS (Ma3)

- Whole step larger than a whole step
- Half step larger than a minor third (mi3)

Use the abbreviations when filling out the interval: mi3 and Ma3.

Key Signature _____

Interval _____

Key Signature _____

Interval _____

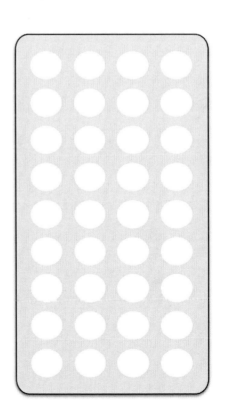

Key Signature _____

Interval _____

Key Signature _____

Interval _____

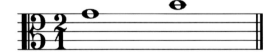

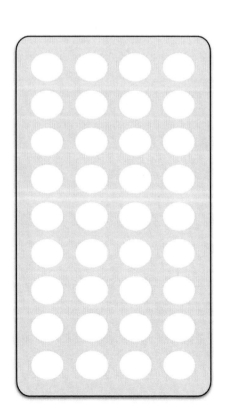

Key Signature _____

Interval _____

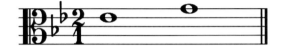

Key Signature _____

Interval _____

Part Three • Thirds

Key Signature _____

Interval _____

Key Signature _____

Interval _____

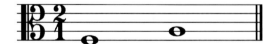

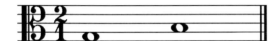

Key Signature _____

Interval _____

Key Signature _____

Interval _____

Key Signature _____

Interval _____

Key Signature _____

Interval _____

Key Signature _____

Interval _____

Key Signature _____

Interval _____

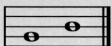

Key Signature _____

Interval _____

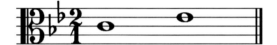

Key Signature _____

Interval _____

Key Signature _____

Interval _____

Key Signature _____

Interval _____

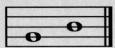
Key Signature _____

Interval _____

Key Signature _____

Interval _____

Key Signature _____

Interval _____

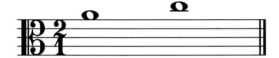

Key Signature _____

Interval _____

Key Signature _____

Interval _____

Key Signature _____

Interval _____

Key Signature _____

Interval _____

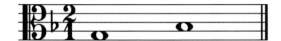

Key Signature _____

Interval _____

Key Signature _____

Interval _____

Key Signature _____

Interval _____

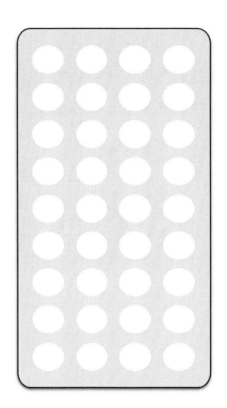

Key Signature _____

Interval _____

Key Signature _____

Interval _____

Key Signature _____

Interval _____

Key Signature _____

Interval _____

Key Signature _____

Interval _____

Key Signature _____

Interval _____

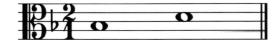

Key Signature _____

Interval _____

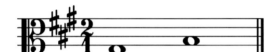

Key Signature _____

Interval _____

Key Signature _____

Interval _____

Key Signature _____

Interval _____

Key Signature _____

Interval _____

Key Signature _____

Interval _____

Part Three • Thirds

Key Signature _____

Interval _____

Key Signature _____

Interval _____

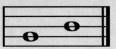

Key Signature _____

Interval _____

Key Signature _____

Interval _____

Key Signature _____

Interval _____

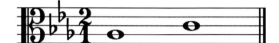

Key Signature _____

Interval _____

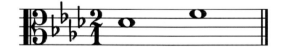

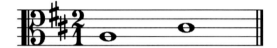

Key Signature _____

Interval _____

─────────────────────────────────

Key Signature _____

Interval _____

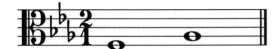

Key Signature _____

Interval _____

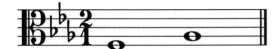

Key Signature _____

Interval _____

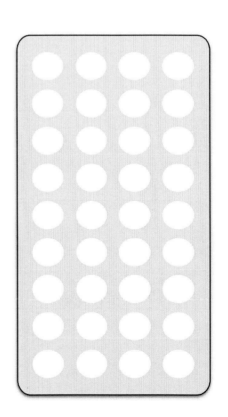

Key Signature _____

Interval _____

Key Signature _____

Interval _____

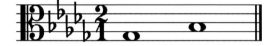

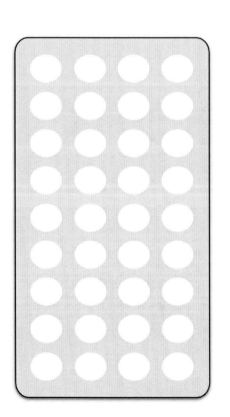

Key Signature _____

Interval _____

Key Signature _____

Interval _____

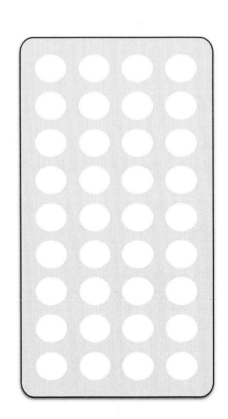

Key Signature _____

Interval _____

Key Signature _____

Interval _____

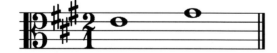

Key Signature _____

Interval _____

Key Signature _____

Interval _____

REVIEW QUESTIONS:

1) Describe how the notes look on the music staff. Are they on lines? Spaces? What is the distance between the lines and/or spaces?

2) Catalog all the fingerings you used in this part. Notice patterns.

3) Describe how the intervals sound to you. Use references to moods, descriptions or songs you recognize.

REVIEW EXERCISE:

Go back and replay all the examples in Part 3 noticing:
• How the interval looks on the staff
• How the fingerings form the intervals
• How the intervals sound like your description

PART FOUR

Fourths

Fourths are four notes apart. You will have two different sizes of fourths.

PERFECT FOURTH (P4)

- Half step larger than a major third (Ma3)
- Half step smaller than an augmented fourth (A4)

AUGMENTED FOURTH (A4)

- Whole step larger than a major third (Ma3)
- Half step larger than a perfect fourth (P4)

Use the abbreviations when filling out the interval: P4 and A4.

Key Signature _____

Interval _____

Key Signature _____

Interval _____

Key Signature _____

Interval _____

Key Signature _____

Interval _____

Key Signature _____

Interval _____

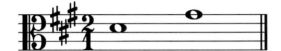

Key Signature _____

Interval _____

Key Signature _____

Interval _____

Key Signature _____

Interval _____

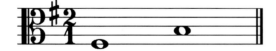

Key Signature _____

Interval _____

Key Signature _____

Interval _____

Key Signature _____

Interval _____

Key Signature _____

Interval _____

Key Signature _____

Interval _____

Key Signature _____

Interval _____

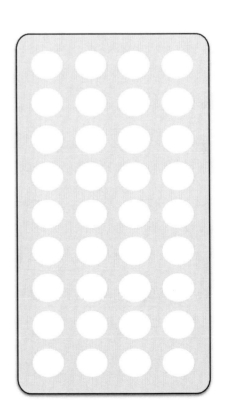

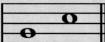

Key Signature _____

Interval _____

Key Signature _____

Interval _____

Key Signature _____

Interval _____

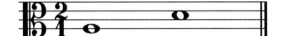

Key Signature _____

Interval _____

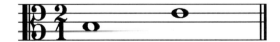

Key Signature _____

Interval _____

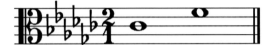

Key Signature _____

Interval _____

Key Signature _____

Interval _____

Key Signature _____

Interval _____

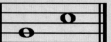 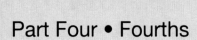

Key Signature _____

Interval _____

Key Signature _____

Interval _____

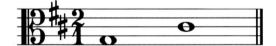

Key Signature _____

Interval _____

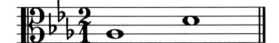

Key Signature _____

Interval _____

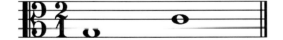

Key Signature _____

Interval _____

Key Signature _____

Interval _____

Key Signature _____

Interval _____

Key Signature _____

Interval _____

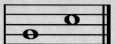

Key Signature _____

Interval _____

Key Signature _____

Interval _____

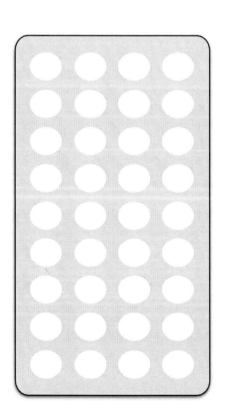

Key Signature _____

Interval _____

Key Signature _____

Interval _____

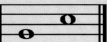

Key Signature _____

Interval _____

Key Signature _____

Interval _____

Key Signature _____

Interval _____

Key Signature _____

Interval _____

Key Signature _____

Interval _____

Key Signature _____

Interval _____

Key Signature _____

Interval _____

Key Signature _____

Interval _____

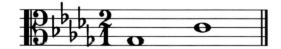

Key Signature _____

Interval _____

Key Signature _____

Interval _____

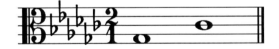

Key Signature _____

Interval _____

Key Signature _____

Interval _____

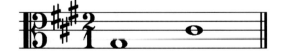

Key Signature _____

Interval _____

Key Signature _____

Interval _____

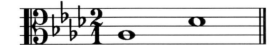

Key Signature _____

Interval _____

Key Signature _____

Interval _____

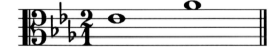

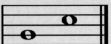

Key Signature _____

Interval _____

REVIEW QUESTIONS:

1) Describe how the notes look on the music staff. Are they on lines? Spaces? What is the distance between the lines and/or spaces?

2) Catalog all the fingerings you used in this part. Notice patterns.

3) Describe how the intervals sound to you. Use references to moods, descriptions or songs you recognize.

REVIEW EXERCISE:

Go back and replay all the examples in Part 4 noticing:

• How the interval looks on the staff

• How the fingerings form the intervals

• How the intervals sound like your description

PART FIVE

Fifths

Fifths are five notes apart. You will have two different sizes of fifths.

DIMINISHED FIFTH (d5)

- Same exact size as an augmented fourth (A4)
- Enharmonic spelling of the augmented fourth (A4)
- Half step smaller than the perfect fifth (P5)

PERFECT FIFTH (P5)

- Half step larger than the augmented fourth (A4)
- Half step larger than the diminished fifth (d5)

Use the abbreviations when filling out the interval: d5 and P5.

Key Signature _____

Interval _____

Key Signature _____

Interval _____

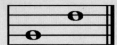

Key Signature _____

Interval _____

Key Signature _____

Interval _____

Key Signature _____

Interval _____

Key Signature _____

Interval _____

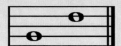

Key Signature _____

Interval _____

Key Signature _____

Interval _____

Key Signature _____

Interval _____

Key Signature _____

Interval _____

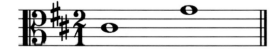

Key Signature _____

Interval _____

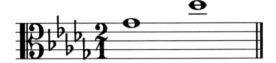

Key Signature _____

Interval _____

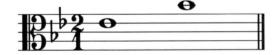

Key Signature _____

Interval _____

Key Signature _____

Interval _____

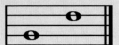

Key Signature _____

Interval _____

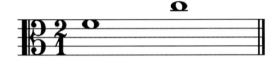

Key Signature _____

Interval _____

Key Signature _____

Interval _____

Key Signature _____

Interval _____

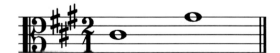

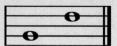 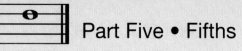

Key Signature _____

Interval _____

Key Signature _____

Interval _____

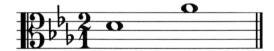

Key Signature _____

Interval _____

Key Signature _____

Interval _____

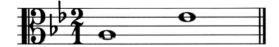

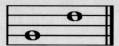

Key Signature _____

Interval _____

Key Signature _____

Interval _____

Key Signature _____

Interval _____

Key Signature _____

Interval _____

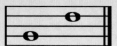 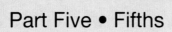
Key Signature _____

Interval _____

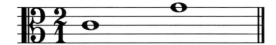

Key Signature _____

Interval _____

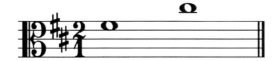

Key Signature _____

Interval _____

Key Signature _____

Interval _____

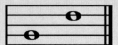

Key Signature _____

Interval _____

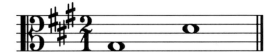

Key Signature _____

Interval _____

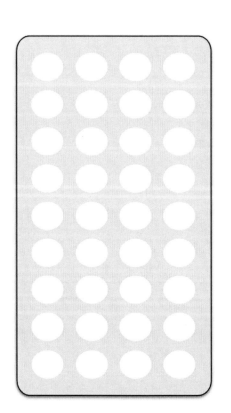

Key Signature _____

Interval _____

Key Signature _____

Interval _____

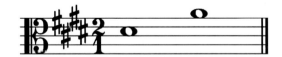

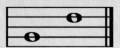

Key Signature _____

Interval _____

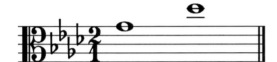

Key Signature _____

Interval _____

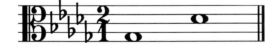

Key Signature _____

Interval _____

Key Signature _____

Interval _____

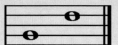

Key Signature _____

Interval _____

Key Signature _____

Interval _____

Key Signature _____

Interval _____

Key Signature _____

Interval _____

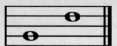 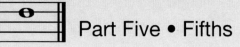

Key Signature _____

Interval _____

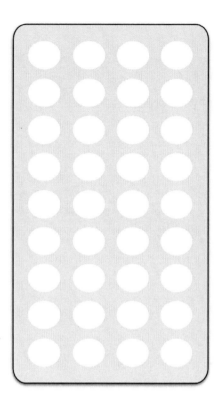

Key Signature _____

Interval _____

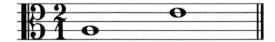

Key Signature _____

Interval _____

Key Signature _____

Interval _____

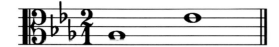

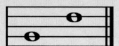
Key Signature _____

Interval _____

Key Signature _____

Interval _____

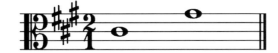

Part 5: Fifths

REVIEW QUESTIONS:

1) Describe how the notes look on the music staff. Are they on lines? Spaces? What is the distance between the lines and/or spaces?

2) Catalog all the fingerings you used in this part. Notice patterns.

3) Describe how the intervals sound to you. Use references to moods, descriptions or songs you recognize.

REVIEW EXERCISE:

Go back and replay all the examples in Part 5 noticing:
- How the interval looks on the staff
- How the fingerings form the intervals
- How the intervals sound like your description

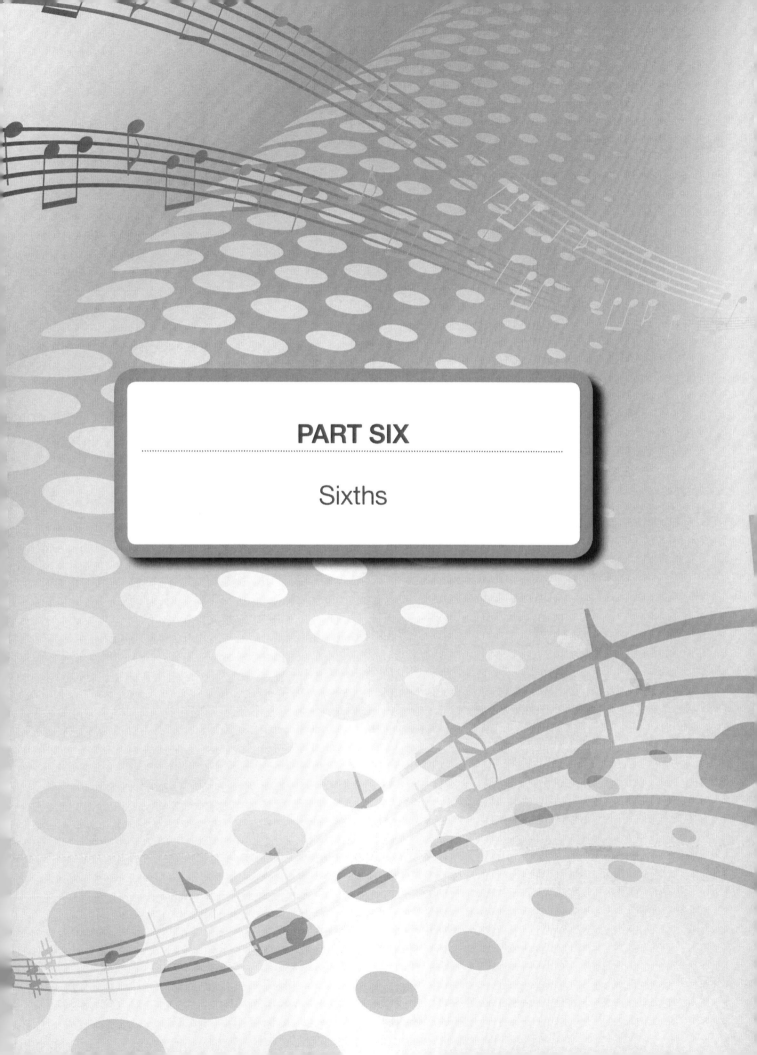

PART SIX

Sixths

Sixths are six notes apart. You will have two different sizes of sixths.

MINOR SIXTH (mi6)

- Half step larger than the perfect fifth (P5)
- Half step smaller than the major sixth (Ma6)

MAJOR SIXTH (Ma6)

- Whole step larger than the perfect fifth (P5)
- Half step larger than the minor sixth (mi6)

Use the abbreviations when filling out the interval: mi6 and Ma6.

Key Signature _____

Interval _____

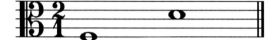

Key Signature _____

Interval _____

Key Signature _____

Interval _____

Key Signature _____

Interval _____

Key Signature _____

Interval _____

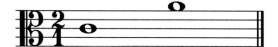

Key Signature _____

Interval _____

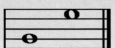

Key Signature _____

Interval _____

Key Signature _____

Interval _____

Key Signature _____

Interval _____

Key Signature _____

Interval _____

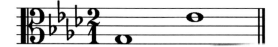

Key Signature _____

Interval _____

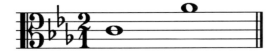

Key Signature _____

Interval _____

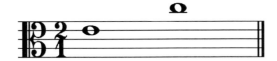

Key Signature _____

Interval _____

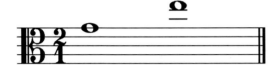

Key Signature _____

Interval _____

Key Signature _____

Interval _____

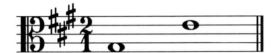

Key Signature _____

Interval _____

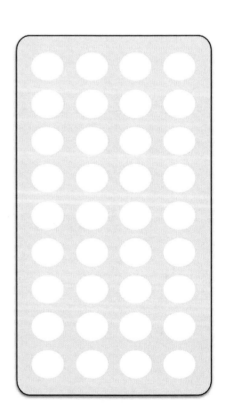

Key Signature _____

Interval _____

Key Signature _____

Interval _____

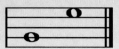

Key Signature _____

Interval _____

Key Signature _____

Interval _____

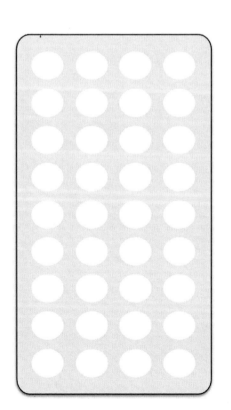

Key Signature _____

Interval _____

Key Signature _____

Interval _____

Key Signature _____

Interval _____

Key Signature _____

Interval _____

Key Signature _____

Interval _____

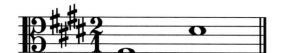

Key Signature _____

Interval _____

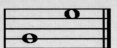

Key Signature _____

Interval _____

Key Signature _____

Interval _____

Key Signature _____

Interval _____

Key Signature _____

Interval _____

Key Signature _____

Interval _____

Key Signature _____

Interval _____

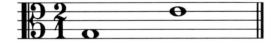

Key Signature _____

Interval _____

Key Signature _____

Interval _____

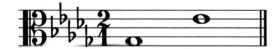

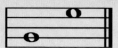

Part Six • Sixths

Key Signature _____

Interval _____

Key Signature _____

Interval _____

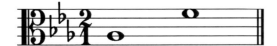

Part 6: Sixths

REVIEW QUESTIONS:

1) Describe how the notes look on the music staff. Are they on lines? Spaces? What is the distance between the lines and/or spaces?

2) Catalog all the fingerings you used in this part. Notice patterns.

3) Describe how the intervals sound to you. Use references to moods, descriptions or songs you recognize.

REVIEW EXERCISE:

Go back and replay all the examples in Part 6 noticing:
- How the interval looks on the staff
- How the fingerings form the intervals
- How the intervals sound like your description

PART SEVEN

Sevenths

Sevenths are seven notes apart. You will have two different sizes of sevenths.

MINOR SEVENTH (mi7)

- Half step larger than the major sixth (Ma6)
- Half step smaller than the major seventh (Ma7)

MAJOR SEVENTH (Ma7)

- Whole step larger than the major sixth (Ma6)
- Half step larger than minor seventh (mi7)

Use abbreviations when filling out the interval: mi7 and Ma7.

Key Signature _____

Interval _____

Key Signature _____

Interval _____

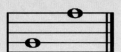

Key Signature _____

Interval _____

Key Signature _____

Interval _____

Key Signature _____

Interval _____

Key Signature _____

Interval _____

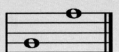

Key Signature _____

Interval _____

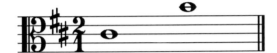

Key Signature _____

Interval _____

Key Signature _____

Interval _____

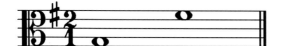

Key Signature _____

Interval _____

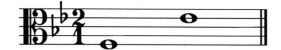

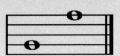

Key Signature _____

Interval _____

Key Signature _____

Interval _____

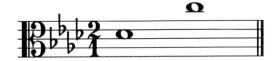

Key Signature _____

Interval _____

Key Signature _____

Interval _____

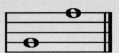

Key Signature _____

Interval _____

Key Signature _____

Interval _____

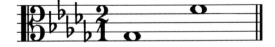

Key Signature _____

Interval _____

Key Signature _____

Interval _____

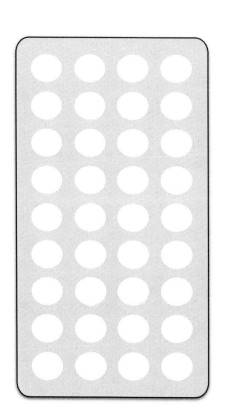

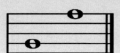

Part Seven • Seventhsrlr

Key Signature _____

Interval _____

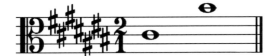

Key Signature _____

Interval _____

Key Signature _____

Interval _____

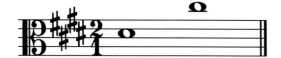

Key Signature _____

Interval _____

Key Signature _____

Interval _____

Key Signature _____

Interval _____

Key Signature _____

Interval _____

Key Signature _____

Interval _____

Part 7: Sevenths

REVIEW QUESTIONS:

1) Describe how the notes look on the music staff. Are they on lines? Spaces? What is the distance between the lines and/or spaces?

2) Catalog all the fingerings you used in this part. Notice patterns.

3) Describe how the intervals sound to you. Use references to moods, descriptions or songs you recognize.

REVIEW EXERCISE:

Go back and replay all the examples in Part 7 noticing:
- How the interval looks on the staff
- How the fingerings form the intervals
- How the intervals sound like your description

PART EIGHT

Octaves

Octaves are eight notes apart. They could be called octaves or perfect eights (P8). It is more common to call them octaves.

OCTAVES

• Half step larger than major seventh (Ma7)

Use the word Octave when filling out the interval.

Key Signature _____

Interval _____

Key Signature _____

Interval _____

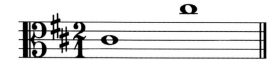

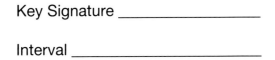

Key Signature _____

Interval _____

Key Signature _____

Interval _____

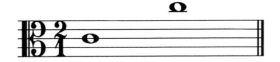

Key Signature _____

Interval _____

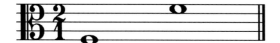

Key Signature _____

Interval _____

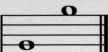

Key Signature _____

Interval _____

Key Signature _____

Interval _____

Part 8: Octaves

REVIEW QUESTIONS:

1) Describe how the notes look on the music staff. Are they on lines? Spaces? What is the distance between the lines and/or spaces?

2) Catalog all the fingerings you used in this part. Notice patterns.

3) Describe how the intervals sound to you. Use references to moods, descriptions or songs you recognize.

REVIEW EXERCISE:

Go back and replay all the examples in Part 8 noticing:

• How the interval looks on the staff

• How the fingerings form the intervals

• How the intervals sound like your description

Congratulations!

You've made it to the end of the workbook!
Go back one more time and play through all
the exercises looking at the fingerboard and
the musical example.

You are now ready to study another position!

Made in United States
North Haven, CT
26 March 2023